I SHOULD HAVE BEEN SIX FEET UNDER

BY: SENSATIONAL LUMMITOR

Book Edited, Designed and Published By:

The Motivational Club (Pty) Ltd
2 De Beer Street
Braamfontein
Johannesburg
2001
Republic of South Africa

Tel: +27 (0) 11 046 9394
Mobile: +27(0) 79 079 2169
E-mail: publish@motivationalclub.co.za
Website: www.motivationalclub.co.za

Author's Contact:

Cell: +27(0) 76 561 4872
E-mail: sensationallummi@gmail.com

ISBN: 9798637204670

TABLE OF CONTENTS

ACKNOWLEDGEMENT

I would like to acknowledge the following people who made it possible for this novel to be a success.

Richard Thomas Mitchel:

If I could be given a chance, certainly I would run for it.
My grandfather left too early while I still needed his love throughout my journey. I love him and if he never existed at all, certainly I wouldn't be here because my mom exists on Earth because of him who has left us.

Essie Semponeng Mitchel:

I would write another novel when I think of all the amazing thing's my grandma has done and still doing for the entire family. She has a golden heart which everyone wishes to have. It is her heart and words of wisdom that brings comfort in distressed souls. I am who I am today because of her. My love for her urges me to be at my level best daily in whatever activity I do.

Josephine Oinah Mitchel:

My mom is more than just a single mom to me, she is my warrior and my strength in times of weakness. She keeps my head up high as I walk towards my success. What she has achieved in life is my wakeup call when I seem to be throwing in the towel. I am who I am today because of her struggles before I could even exist on this Earth.

Freddie Mitchel:

My uncle has always been there for me since day one. His presence in my life and the knowledge he has taught me as a male has influenced me to be a better person. His success is one of the factors that pushes me to my absolute best daily.

CHAPTER I

Each and every little soul living in this miserable world has a story to tell. One of those stories came into light when trees would lose their leaves to the ground, during the season of autumn. The birth of an ambiance, destined for great things in life is the baby lying in the manger, 'Sensational Lummitor'. Memories were indeed created during my childhood, everyone in the Mitchel family would sing ululations and admiration melodies of astuteness.

At first, it was entirely pleasant, I lived in harmony under the palm of he who defended me even at times when he knew I was wrong. (Giggles).... I guess I was spoiled by my grandfather. That alone was never perceived as a good thing by my aunt. She would say my grandfather is feeding me with rotten seeds, of which eventually will grow within me. In every household, the teachings that your family offers you, is seen by your moral behavior as an individual. Out of all his grandchildren, I was the chosen one, wow!

My grandpa, never lived at home, he spent his days in the bushes looking after his cows. We as his grandchildren out of love would offer our time to assist and look after the cows, urging him to go home and rest. My love for him is exceedingly admirable and has no bonds. I am a young soul dressed in powerful blankets by the ancestors and everybody in the family looks up to me. Despite being one of the third generations of the Mitchel grandchildren, I am the feet driving the first generation into the right path. The world is upon my shoulders, the future of the family is perceived directly from all of my actions but I don't know of such yet.

(Sigh)…I would be blamed for all the intense moment I encountered with my fellow cousins. That was part of growing up I guess, nonetheless all the memories we created are all to be cherished.

My childhood in general was convoluted. All of those teachings, I will apprize and apply them in order to make tomorrow a better day than today. My family cared so much for me to an extent that I thought "They were taking away my childhood". When I think back about: the tears, heartache and laughter I endured, I start realizing their love which i failed to see as a child.

I still don't understand how I managed to survive what could have been a painful unbearable incident. What really transpired that day truly cannot be defined. At all times before I ran away from home, I would peep through the corners of the household to be certain that nobody stops me while I am on the run. That day I don't know why I never checked the coast, I guess my life was on the line and God still wanted me on this Earth. As I climbed up a pole, I slid and fell hard on a nail spearing through my throat. I can still see the pole draped in dark red blood, my esophagus loosing so much blood. If my grandfather never went to check up on the cows, surely I would be six feet under.

Several number of incidents occurred that might have brought my existence on Earth to an early end. The greatest judge of them all my Lord God saved me from all the instances I would have died and I could never thank him better than to visit him daily through prayer.

Crying was not an option; it would make the situation worse than do justice, nonetheless I missed him so much when he was at hospital. He was way too sick and I am to blame. I have been given a gift to see things that will occur in future, yet, I took those dreams lightly and never shared my dreams with elders. Only if I shared my dreams with them, maybe I could have spared my grandfather a year or two on this Earth. Why didn't I say something that morning when he fell from his bed, which I had seen in my dreams?

I seemed to be running out of time, but now that I think about it, I could have said something about the cow that had to be sold perhaps the unfortunate outcome wouldn't have occurred.

A brahma bull that was red in color if I remember correctly, if only we sold it maybe I could have saved my grandpa from the suffering he endured and brought him back to a healthy life. The day my life as a child shuttered finally arrived, I always knew it would come, but that day came as a surprise. It was Sunday morning, 07 October 2007, exactly ten hours a voice from afar yelling" Shimita tlamo", meaning come here and I rushed without knowing why, my grandma was washing her face and she said, "Your grandfather wants you to loosen his feet" I held his feet and made them straight, out of shock they bend again, I could see the look on my eyes with the thought that this is some sort of a joke. When I think of it now, I just become speechless and still cannot come into conclusions of the cause of such. Minutes had gone by since I had left my Grandpa's chamber and at that juncture I was sitting with my siblings on the stoop enjoying fresh cuisine prepared by my aunt. (Crying)… I heard a loud scream from my aunt, I thought upon myself that she was disturbing grandpa's sleep.

The crying sound of my aunt was so high that I couldn't take it, though I never knew the real cause as to why she was crying. As I finished eating, I tried to go into the kitchen to wash my dish, out of disbelieve I was restricted and ridiculous excuses would be made to make me understand. It was around 13 hours and my aunt were cleaning, "What on Earth was going on", I asked myself? Somehow I managed to go into the house without anyone noticing, as I went into my room I peeped through my grandpa's room, I saw his head covered with a blanket and I knew he was no more, he is now with the Great Judge looking over me.

I always asked myself if I was the reason behind his untimely death.

If I had shared all of those dreams I had about him would he have lived longer? I will never forgive myself as I always pinpoint his death to my egocentric behavior, but I was young, I understand. Now that I am old I think of all of the ways I had a chance to change the outcome of my miserable childhood, but it's already too late.

My heart drips red blood flowing like a valley along with tears of regret.

As always when one is down and cannot get up- it is expected that everyone around you especially those whom are of the same blood as you assist and comforts you in times of sorrow and heartache. Sadly I cannot say such about him. Who is he that I am referring to? Isn't he of any importance to me, so many questions left unanswered, but I have accepted, though my temperament is still feeling the pain caused by him (my dad). On the 12th of October 2007, the night before we laid my grandfather to his final resting place, dad made empty promises saying he would be there to catch my tears as I see my grandfather being buried. He never did and that was the last time I saw him.

I was affected emotionally; I never thought I would get over it, so much has happened and I don't understand why I never shed a tear at the burial of my grandfather. I guess anxiety took its course and blocked all of my feelings. Despite everything, I couldn't remain firm, my eyes just turned dark red and blood flowed through my eyes. The sadness that was on my face as I saw my grandmother getting out of that hearse covered in blankets really shattered my heart.

I guess that's the moment I developed strong love for her. She became the sword that eliminates every bad deed I ever encountered in my life. I had always been afraid but Essie (my grandmother) invested so much in me that I became steady and rigid on the ground.

I had always asked myself where she got all the courage from, but now it makes sense that grandpa and God were her strength when she felt weak.

For some reasons, I pinpoint the emotions I portrayed at the graveyard as the mere reason why I am now living such a miserable life.
All it had to take was for rain to start and that was not eco-friendly at all. I was not myself so I started running in such a weather condition. Everyone in the family was stressed thinking of my wellbeing as they knew I was badly affected. I hid in the backyard of the house thinking of my grandfather with the rain falling hard on my soft skin. My pure heart turned evil, my blood thickened and I placed the blame on other people for every bad thing that transpired in my life.

Perhaps I was too egocentric, thinking that the world along with its creatures owe me something. Truth be told, I was raised well and I could still remember despite being a selfish person that in this life I am not entitled to anything. Nevertheless, I still deserve to live a happy and healthy lifestyle without hurting anyone.

CHAPTER II

Evil intentions go through my mind as I walk down the memory lane of my life. I concluded that I was staring at some movie and one day it will all end. It really hit me hard thinking timeously that it would all end in just a blink, but life amazed me. It amazed me in many ways; my love life a complete disaster, I tried fixing the situation but another wound opened. I couldn't believe the logical thinking of my mind as I was only eighteen years of age, but thought like an old man. Always thinking of the level of maturity on my fellow peers at school, getting all worked up by immature behaviors.

Nobody understood why I was always moody and nobody understood the type of a teenager I was because I always behaved differently from my fellow peers. I really found it hard to accept the life I was living but at the end of the day I had to be strong, man up and take control of the situation. Life is like a journey that awaits you from the very same moment you arrive on Earth and it's expected from your guardians to raise you accordingly to, guide you throughout so that you will be able to make the best choices when you arrive at a self-governing podium of life.

I owe it to my grand mom Essie for making me the proud young man I have become today, it is because of her teaching that makes me special and unique, she taught me how to respect, love, and honor and more importantly she taught me how to be brave and creative. Essie is the heroin of the village I live in; many families see her as the mother of the village. I remember the day the mother of the village shared her real life story of how she saved Lames life when all hope was gone from the mother of the little boy, but by the mercy of God and the mother of the villages belief the boy was saved from death.

I can never ask for a better role model than my grand mom that is why I follow in her footsteps, which is why I have a fragile heart .My heart is unstable it knows how to stress frequently not because I let it, but nobody can control what the heart feels. I truly wish I had a medicine to cure the way people misuse my heart, by bringing tears to my eyes and misery into my life. In life we ought to meet a few wrong people so that we can get strong spiritually, physical and mentally.   This is essential because when everything is said and done we will then be blessed with the right person.

In life, we ought to use our past into better use. We should not forget about the hardships of our past, so that when we grow old we can look back into the past to improve ourselves. I seem to struggle with the handling of matters of the heart (which is feelings for someone); without having any control of my emotions I channel through the deepest emotions of my wretched temperament caused by my loved ones.

What is love? I don't really understand it. My mind is not at ease, I struggle to calm my burning heart because there are many infuriating emotions deep within me. I am not a two faced type of person but the kind of life I was offered by the GREAT ONE is in some way a two-faced kind of life. I should never get too excited. Tears of hurt flow roughly on my cheeks, too much happiness always leads to sadness at the end of the day. I solemnly said to myself "No matter what comes along my way be it a good at the last degree I will always uphold my expressions of gratitude".
I just care too much about how it becomes every time it's left wounded either by too much excitement or by a mademoiselle. I used to be a big time trouper, used to agate around with women's feelings. I truly regret how I acted towards women. It has come to my acknowledgement that a person of which holds the physiognomies of a female is a very distinctive ambiance and one who would become my soul mate at the end of time.

I have the temperament of a bird which is pure and it does not care what kind of a person you are, everyone deserves to have me in their life because I am a blessing, I come in a form of a gift from the Deity.

Even though at times I am a bit grumpy as my soul burns deep within. This has come into light because of an uncontrollable frame of mind triggered by a woman. The love which I offered with an open and pure heart, the love that I offered with a burning heart, the love that I thought it was real and better than everyone else but I never realized that my love would be abused. Deep down inside I solemnly told myself that the love I offer is needed by everyone. Each and every time after the heart has been smashed by their loved ones the first thing that we all tell ourselves is that" I'll never fall in love again". It is a normal feeling that everyone who has been through such a commitment will feel.

I'm sitting here today in this dark room all by myself thinking about all the possibilities that I could turn my life around, without any direction of where my life is heading to. I daily think of turning my life around yet there are always stumbling blocks to my objectives, if it's not the world then it's my emotions from my past. What if I am the real cause of all this misery I'm living, who knows? I don't know. My life is really complicated as I walk through the complexities of love.

All I ever wanted was to have my own peace of mind, to contemplate upon my existence. There is nothing as painful as loving someone who does not return back the love you initially gave from day one of meeting. When I think about it, tears of sadness roll down my cheeks as people kept on telling me to let go because at the end I will be heartbroken but my stubbornness acted as a stumbling block to a great extent that I concluded it was nothing but jealousy talking.

In life we meet two types of people, the first type is the one who comes into your life to make a positive impact and does only good things in your life and it's hard to let them go. The other type is the one who comes into your life with the intention of destroying you without giving you any sign that their motive is nothing other than to destroy you.

It almost feels like there is a dark cloud hanging over me whereby I'm being denied the chance of living a happy life with my love. Recalling the words, "Have you ever loved someone so bad, but will never be loved now and not in a million years". What could I possibly do to be in her arms when I'm feeling scrawny? How can I think of such when I'm perceived as nothing in her eyes? What can I possibly do that's what I ask myself? A tear in my eyes symbolizing the amount of hurt that I went through is unbearable, simply because of a lady.

The choices I made in my life brought about certain challenges, that of which I could get through and some being too hard to conquer. If there is any teenager in the world, who experienced the worst life, that would be me. I have experienced the worst pain ever, lost so many things in life, some which I thought would be mine forever or be part of me for a single moment called forever. As I ruminate posterior on the past I had endured, I seem to appreciate what God had done for me for the past 18 years of my life. Each and every time someone closed the chapter of our lives; someone else opened the door in my dark room and offered me another chance at love. It is for this reason, I thank the gigantic Noble for every little thing he offered me, without him I would have never made it this far. My existence in this Earth would be extinct by now if it hadn't been for his protection.

CHAPTER III

As we grow, we happen to say our final goodbyes to our friends and loved ones. That is just the sad truth about life. As the time to say goodbye approaches; our souls are left wounded, saddened and full of tears. One thing I have learnt in life is the fact that we ought to appreciate every moment in all circumstances, be it that we are offered more or little, what matters is that we got something and its worth to be appreciated. I still appreciate the little time I had spent with my dearest souls. I have acknowledged the fact that teenagers at times make vows to their loved ones saying that the love existing deep within will last forever. What we don't realize is that nothing lasts forever, because there is a time to love and a time to let go.

Lately I am scared for my burning heart as it is too fragile to endure hurt from a loved one. Furthermore, I am too kind to be getting ill-treated from those I try to share my heart with. In a simple explanation, I would say am not getting the love I know I deserve. I am so scared of what my heart might end up doing because I feel like it is burning with a fury of flames burning at an extremely hot rate that I can't even measure its temperature. If I were to estimate its temperature, surely it would reach thousands of Celsius in degrees.

If I could tell a lie I would say this is my first time feeling like this, but truth be told I've felt this way before only that now it is stronger than before because there's someone new in my life. I want to be part of your daily routine, I want to be everything you would ever want on this planet, I need you to need me more than the way I need you because it would feel right. Days come and go, season's change, and year's change too but my love for a lady never changes, and the heart will remain constant forever because it is kind, it loves and most especially it knows how to appreciate.

I need to understand why people break my heart but I seem to be failing to reach a conclusion with the real reason why many people I embrace have so much hate for me. If there is something that I am most certain about in my life is that I am a special soul sent from all heaven skies to change the lives of the lost souls. When I say lost souls I am simply talking about those who seem to be trapped in the dark and cannot see a way out but now that I am in the picture I seem to have a way out to help those lost souls.

This is what I always tell myself that I am destined for big things that await me in the long run, but fate seems to have brought it earlier than I expected. I am given a chance to improve the lives of others, I am not a billionaire and I have no cent here with me, but I am improving the lives of other people. I have learnt one thing about life, which is everyone is gifted or I could say God gave us different talents and gifts which is for this reason I say that I am blessed to have a heart that cares and tears apart when someone is experiencing pain of some kind. Even though at times the goodness of my heart would be treated like a complete idiot I am still proud of myself, I vividly remember the day when a very close friend of mine told me "I am very sick", her eyes were filled with nothing but tears of pain and out of the goodness of my heart I brought her some medication, instead of thanking me she called me names.

How can someone who is sick say, "are you crazy, buying me medicine whilst you should have bought me airtime". For a moment I got startled by such an oblivious behavior, in my opinion when someone buys medicine for their loved ones it is an intriguing moment and a day to be cherished but that was not the case for my association with Laila. Teenagers at the latest stage of their teenage hood they seem to be more pre-occupied with their own ideas about what is morally right or wrong and that is defined as ethics in broad accounting terms.

That is simply how I perceive teenagers, because they fail to think out of the box which simply means they are their own stumbling block to their creativity and logical sense of humor.

The goodness of my heart makes it much easier for me to think out of the box. It is not such a bad thing to give thanks to the people who have broken my heart as they are the ones who have turned me into such a loving guy. The only time you can say you know what love is in my perspective is only when you've endured tears of hurt and when your heart has been wounded by the one you trust. This is why I am saying I know what love is because I have endured more pain brought up by the ones I trusted.

I live in a city full of suffering of which the extent of the misery cannot be absconded. There seems to be no way I can escape this kind of lifestyle. I have lost all hope and the only thing for me to do is to surrender all my flaws to the Lord God, because he is the only one who has never turned his back on me and he will never do such. I am a candle shining in the dark and I seem to be trying by all means to light up the dark room in which my friends lay in. In all my living years, each and every soul that I have encountered never resisted help, even those who were egomaniacs.

My peers seem to think that I behave like a child, but truth be told they are all wrong. It is for this reason why teenage kids don't understand me because I befriend old people who know a lot about life.

I fail to understand the level of intellectual intelligence of my peers as they still think life is a fun thing but, well, I can tell life is a very difficult pill to swallow. The kind of life that I am living is difficult to establish whether I am really a teenager or an adult because of the high capacity level of thinking I have.

I know how to accept pain in my life, because my heart has tasted all kinds of pain a human being can feel. It truly changed me into a monster. Nowadays, I have a strange feeling when it comes to the nature of women as I seem to be embracing hate upon them, and they deserve it. Perhaps it is not my words but my infuriating heart as it is shattered but I trust in the Lord God that he will be with me along this journey because in him I trust that this uncalled for remarks will be eliminated and my heart to be restored to what it was before pain embraced itself in my life.

The love I know I deserve will finally come and when it comes I will know nothing more than to give thanks to the only heavenly father, because it would be the blessing that he kept for me my entire life. I really thought for a moment that the lady whose name is Shelda was the real blessing I would be gifted with. It was love at first sight beginning of 2014 when I first saw her, when my first thoughts were that the lady with the red and black outfit would be my girl in the days to come and would in turn be my wife.
I never believed in those words as we never had time to sit and talk it through but when October the 13th approached I believed in the words I said earlier in the year. "Now that I have found you I want to stop seeing other girls as I need to focus all my attention on you" that is what I said that day. We endured sweet, honesty and fell deeply in love whenever we met all we could do is to wave each other smiles no matter who was around, she never cared all she cared about was me. Life was sweet back then, I wish I could relieve all those past memories I shared with Shelda and I wish all the dreams I had about her would all turn out to be true in reality. Never have I dreamt like this before that I even lost count of how many times she appeared in my dreams.

Everybody has their own flaws and so do I. I am not a saint that is why I also go astray in life, but at the end of the day I find my way into the straight line.

I have met them all but I have never met a soul who happened to be more precious than that ever smiling beauty queen who solemnly taught me how to smile. It happens to be a true saying when I say I find love during the month of October as 2015 history repeated itself.

Love is a crazy thing, nobody understands what it is, until you experience hurt, shame and most of all up until you lose what you once had.

I lost Shelda and after some time Princess opened the door to the dark room Shelda left me in. Princess made her presence felt in my life and my heart started glooming with butterflies. When people say life is a burden I lugubriously assume they have not made peace with their past because every day a new door opens as the other one closes in our everyday life and that is a direct reference to my love life.

CHAPTER IV

The word "life" itself is one of those paramount journeys that we happen to partake in our everyday life. We go through obstacles, which at times seems to be impossible to overcome. My life has been posed with many challenges but instead of throwing in the towel, I put in superfluous work to change the circumstances surrounding me. I am a lost soul who waits to be hoarded by the loveliness of the Deity himself. The only thing taking its course at this very own juncture- is greediness and selfishness of which I don't understand where it comes from.

A helping hand is within reach but those who have to be saved are not pulling up their weights to be saved. I am a matriculate of 2016 in Hillside Private School (HPS) striving for excellence of which everyone should feel the same…. but this is not the case and there are several aspects that support my statement. During school terms, the management alerted us that we would embark on winter school during the holidays, thriving for better outcomes at the end of the year.

It is now Sunday morning, days later, as mom helps me pack my bags before she leaves for a meeting in Johannesburg. I am overexcited as I wait for Monday morning with the idea that I would be leaving for the camp. I made a phone call to my granny as I wanted her to give me a word of advice on how I should take care of myself in the outside world far away from family.

The day had finally arrived, everyone was ready to head into the trip, the excitement was extra-ordinary and our faces were all filled with the best smiles which have never been seen before. We said goodbyes to our families and waited for our transport in great anticipation. Some of us never travelled on that road, thus it became one hell of an experience.

The journey was too short but the memories created along the road lasts forever. Along the way as we made a few stops, we went miles away from the taxi and started taking pictures as memories like this only happen once.

As we arrived to the Ubhejani Lodge, the boys were too excited about the place, we were at ease and harmony with the place. What about the girls? Why are they excluded from the thrill we experienced? Yes, you've guessed it right; their expectations were too high and couldn't be met by the management.

Very ludicrous manners were reserved during the summer season of which HPS managed to put measures into place to strive for better matric results comparing with the previous year. At the beginning it was all sweet everyone was excited they wanted to do something with their lives, they were all eager to get an education they deserved.
Everything was running smoothly up until complaints of silliness was made considering the sleeping places we were offered compared with the roof that was offered to the teachers. The people who offered us a roof to lie under for those 13 days of camp began to realize that some of us were greedy, selfish and had no heart to give thanks were it was due. My heart was torn into pieces after realizing that within a few minutes of arrival every one that was carrying the name of HPS already had been holding a bad reputation concerning the fact that we represent the school's name (Hillside Private School).

All of this had been brought about because of a learner who had no virtuous setting. I remember the comment of the principal (Mr. Maumee) after witnessing huge amounts of disrespect from certain learners saying "if you are not happy with what is offered you are more than welcome to pack your bags and wait for the taxi which will take you back home".

While everyone expected the principal to be experiencing the   worst grieve ever, the man had a positive energy flowing right through his veins and everyone who was present at the scene thought he was strong. To my surprise my friend (Menlo) pert me in the back and said "take a close look at how calm the principal is, I can assure you he has a plan in mind of how to deal with the difficult ones, watch the space", just then all my mind could think of was how the principal plans to deal with the people who tried by all means to paint the school with a bad name. The wise words of comfort rendered by Mr. Maumee to every student's ears managed to calm all of us down as we feared our educational trip would last for a short while.

Every time the principal opened his mouth already my soul was ready for the judicious words as they were at all times comforting. The principal stood tall and let no victimization of any kind bring him down as he strived to overcome the stupid challenges he faced with empty minded people. Obstacles strengthen us and tests how far we are willing to go as we try to overcome them. It matters not who you are but what exists in your mind as challenges embraces itself defines you.

In my perspective, people who prefer shortcuts than challenging problems head on don't really end well or become the best they can be. Those souls, who preferred to take the easy way out during the camp, are now in areas outside the school premises. Under such circumstances, my heart is saddened. To an inordinate magnitude, I tried to talk to our principal about the situation of my fellow peers but I came out with nothing.

I am just a small boy who feels remorseful for other people despite the circumstances that led to the situation. A class that is known to be of thirty people was only left with twelve and we were the ones considered to care for our future. That never gave me the opinion that we were more superior to others, NO!

This circumstance was brought about because we never disturbed the learning lessons during the camp. When life gives you a broken chair, you are due to sit on it and then at a later stage of life try by all means to make yourself sit in that very same chair comfortably. It is a fact, the kind of seed you plant for yourself, in the near future you will be the one enjoying the benefits. The story of my life is that I always put an effort into my academics and already I have faced so many challenges that I thought I would never surpass. Demon's and witchcraft were in play throughout the grade 12's winter school trip, which is why my peers were so apprehensive for their lives. I might be erroneous, I might be veracious, but my judgment does not really matter. What really matters most is the hard lesson I learned from all the events that have occurred.

Without recognizing how expedient and severe my life was, I am in deep sensations, feeling repentant. To a certain extent, I judge matric as a grade that takes away everything from a person. Twenty succeed (2016) became cruel; it took away my freedom and soul from the rest of my family. I have been encumbered with great exertion of which I thought it would be impossible to surpass. I never threw in the towel but I strived and kept pushing as hard as I could until I had no power within me to continue. I lived by the principle that I will work hard, for as long as I saw the sun rise and see the day disappearing. I knew that the effort I put into my work will pay off in the end. Hard decisions had to be made, whereby I ended up deciding on the fact that my school work takes priority, i denied myself fun in order to enjoy the merits in the long run. According to my own judgment, it seemed to be the easiest verdict I could ever embark on. The hardest question I kept in mind was whether I would be able to surpass the challenges that are yet to come?

For a moment I paused, thought of the choices I had made over and over again.

In an ultimate prayer I said "Dear Lord, help me surpass the greatest challenge I am about to partake, for I am nothing and powerless to overcome this alone!"

The life that I am living now couldn't have been any better if it weren't for the Lord God who always walks with me everywhere I go. It is for this reason, I trust in him.

All the heartaches and the stresses that I currently endure will be worth it. I will drive luxury cars, build a mansion and most importantly provide a good healthy life for the generation to come for my family. I will be able to tell Sensational junior about all the heartaches I endured to get to where I am now.

CHAPTER V

Factual adoration never expires, be it that the binary ambiances spend a month of Sundays away respectively from each other or not. If we could look into the deepest soul of a human being who loves for real, the love discernible would be esoteric without a blink of an eye. That alone dear colleagues and vestals, I wish it was possible as we would become alert of the real mother nature of our emotional state. When voluminous individuals altered the expression "FOREVER", I lugubriously assumed I would certainly not be one of those entities. However, now that I have perceived it all, the entire bond I share with her is extremely awe-inspiring. Connecting with you has brought a transformation of assertiveness and I have no reason to hesitate when I say a knight in shining amour has brought itself in an early childhood.

Endlessly I will apprize and honor the gift that I was consecrated with. Nonetheless, that of which I wish to keep forever has taken a different route in life leaving my soul and all of me in disbelief. I have learned the greatest lesson that nothing will remain un-altered, no matter how awesome it is, I will acquaint and always judge it to be a fair hour of ecstasy. Does the word secret still have an evocative meaning if it is told? What was meant to be kept in a cage flowed through the world's ears.

In every relationship trust, honor and respect remains to be the fundamental norm, which acts as a conjunction between binary ambiances. Without it "future" can never be reached or seen nearby. Dear Lord I beg of your indulgence to purify my heart. The actions that will be performed by me let it be that of which satisfies and brings elation into your eyes. In hopes that the little prayer I just surrendered to God will bring a great transformation in my love life.

It is for this reason that I was never blessed nor given a good foundation about the love story. I am not perfect; I have sinned, became the reason behind tormented temperaments of those who believed in me. The greatest failure I have ever encountered was disappointing the women whom would mother my kids and prepare a good meal to satisfy the stomach.

How would I have known that she was a devil in disguise? She was beautiful and I told her the deepest secret of my life. I lost everything I had and my future went down the drain. She was the one I thought would forever be mine no matter what but I drove a spear straight in her heart. At that juncture, I knew that time was up, that alone was all the time God had planned for our connection. I knew a different meaning of death that it was not only about being promoted into another world. It can be known as the point in life whereby communication between you and the other comes to an end forever. There is nothing I can do but accept, though it would be hard to get past the situation. I try so hard to think of the good things that are happening in my life, but I find no amusement of any sort.

Life is hard comrades, yet I am still here surviving the worst grief interminably. As I lay on my bed weakened to the last degree, had given up on life. As I waited for the heaven skies phone call, one from my ancestors and God himself with teary eyes. A monarch right before my face out of nowhere commands "wake up and kneel down before your Lord God in a prayer and alert him of everything you in need of and he shall provide". A sparkling star shines right through my eyes as I am given a better chance at life to plant seeds that of which I will enjoy in the near future. I have been given an acquiescence to be the shining star that brightens the room filled with lost souls left in the dark. I recall and re-assess, God takes away things that we are not in need off and then re-invests with more than what we hoped we would be in possession off.

I am sometimes amused by people's reaction to change as I perceive it is an aspect that improves the social well-being of a human being. I am not trying to act as a judge but on my perspective change is good. However, we have to bear in mind that people see things differently and that is what makes us unique in our respective ways. A relationship is an evolving process of our lives that teaches us how to hold on tight to circumstances that are detrimental to our wellbeing. Happiness and heartache always take turns in our lives because it is part of growing up into a better soul. Without heartache, we would never appreciate happiness endured in relationships. All the above contention, brings me to conclude my sentiment that even though all of the women I have shared a heart with have all let me down, I am still keen on seeing how my love life will be when tomorrow comes.

All of my loved ones are the reason behind my love for nature. I would stare at the beauty of the stars in deep thoughts. Sometimes I smiled as I felt at ease with the atmosphere around me but also I cried considering aspects of misery I had endured. At times I got so mad at my loved one that I even planned for a massive revenge so that she would feel the pain she caused me. Left alone trapped in manacles in the bushes near a Lion's den, could I survive what could be a massive massacre? I think long and hard. Though in mind whilst I thought about vengeance I also thought about the long term effect it will have on both binary souls. Do I want to be a reason behind a broken soul? Is this how I was raised to act in the most cruel manner to my loved ones or any person surrounding me?

That alone brought a change of heart and I fell in love with myself. I would truly say thinking of the well-being of other people brings my emotions and all of me in a world of comfort, this is because I have been taught a saying in my language that reads "Motho ke motho ka batho" which means according to my understanding that a human being can only be a human because of people in his surrounding.

I could never let my soul be filled with emotions that are not well or that will not build me in any way for tomorrow.

Comrades vengeance brings about hatred and forces one to take drastic actions but in-turn all will be regretted. Speaking from experience, truth is the saying that reads "Let bygones be bygones", we as wrongdoers in our own lives have to abide by it, in order to save ourselves from many things. When tomorrow comes we would have escaped the outrageous nature of life, death, injury, and worst case scenario's involving the law.
Whoever acted in a manner that never set well with my soul, I choose to let God take action upon them. I do this because I trust his judgment and that he has a better plan for me. He will never let the devil indulge himself in his temple (that being my body). Though truth is I am not a proud young man, my actions sometimes are just too much to consume. That is just a mere truth that I don't need anyone to tell as I know myself better than anyone else.

There lives a soul with a heart that's truly shattered into small pieces, and I did the damage. Anger and bitterness are the root cause of why she feels less like a woman. Her soul has been emotionally brutalized by he who says he loves her. Is love meant to take away from us? If what I am giving her is love then surely I don't want to love any longer. The reason for that is because it is not good for any human being living on this Earth.

Her identical twin (Segoe) is always supportive, at every epoch I turn to her even when I am wrong she defends me. The promises I made to her about her sister is upon the level of her expectations on the man who should put a ring on her sister's finger. In her eyes, nobody seemed fit to do such than me. Each and every day I cry, Segoe does not know how painful it is to consume words that depersonalize a human being, to an extent that her eyes become dark red, no amount of words can describe the pain she is feeling in her heart.

There is no permanent impeccable soul. The most ultimate prayer proves our guiltiness as we indulge ourselves in sin. It is for this reason why we live each day to bring shame in the eyes of our loved ones, without a cause. The pain that we cause them is truly unendurable and eventually it shall push them away. My heart wrings of dark red blood, I feel my body shutting down every solitary instant due to my wrongdoings which have a negative effect on my wellbeing.

Thatoe is disappointed by my comportments, trusted me too much that I wouldn't kill an insect or do any harm on any living thing. All of that had to change in a blink of an eye. Too much expectation led to greatest disappointment and misery.

I wish I had all the right lyrics or verses to recite to Thatoe, notifying her how ashamed I am for my irresponsible behavior. I am always lying on my bed thinking hard whether she will catch me as I fall from the ninth floor or turn a blind eye. Whatever action she choose to take upon the situation, she would be well within her rights as I stand still waiting for the punishment she decides to give me. The horrific experience I put her through is in fact a detrimental aspect on a human beings mind and soul. I wish I could put my heart before her just only to show her that the pain she feels is the same pain I feel every day. I would do this just to prove to her how much I long for her presence in my despondent existence. I lie in bed in deep thoughts of her, wishing my expression of regret will be recognized. I would be over the moon if such happens and I will apprize and honor being a new soul before her in a sense that I will be brand new and start afresh.

I have to swallow my pride and accept that I have a problem. Whatever it is that lies deep within me is one that needs expert's intervention such as psychologists and counselors.

This is one of the extreme measures I am willing to take in order to gain back her trust and respect. I wish she could see just how much I strive to become a better person.

I have to stop pinning the blame on people and start acknowledging when I am wrong. Though I still think if it had not been for the rough treatment I received from her, we wouldn't be where we are now. Instead, we would be enjoying each other's company. I can never lose Thatoe simply because of my immoral behavior and that is the reason why I am taking decisive measures to step forward and be a better man.

CHAPTER VI

The best kind of interaction between mortals is not seen when they are tangibly next to each other. People can be far away from each other and still communicate like brothers and sisters. It is possible through social networks of all kinds (WhatsApp, Facebook, etc...) All it takes is good communication that brings both bashes at ease, as long as there is mutual respect in between. What is it that everyone needs? I know and I am certain that it is a friend. A friend is needed in every distinct life to assist the other in both the decent and the wicked times. He or she should be able to stand by you and have the courage to look at circumstances that seem impossible. For me, that is the kind of an ambiance I can mix with because I would find it easy to talk to him or her soul to soul.

There is no relationship that has no ups and downs. Sometimes our soul mates make us do some self-introspection in order to find answers that of which will satisfy your needs and wants in a relationship. For me, even though I have been in many relationships, I never defined what it really was but Kaithline at one point pushed my emotions over the edge and made me question myself "What is it that combines two souls?" though I was not at all certain about what it truly was. Throughout the course of my existence I've been practicing it with different kinds of fair creatures but could not define what a relationship was. In just a blink of a second, there was a sudden and a drastic change of heart. All it had to take was my heart to feel bitter and torn into pieces. I never thought I could get over that feeling as I was hurt and my heart draped cold red blood. My eyes would look dark red and the pain helped me with a meaningful explanation of what a relationship is and what it truly means with a single thought in mind, that being the future endeavors.

A relationship is a bond between two souls who are able to surpass obstacles that come their way. It is all about thinking about two people all at once without forgetting about yourself as an individual. Moreover, I would say it is about communicating about all that is good and bad and finding answers to hard questions you cannot overcome alone.

Furthermore, it is about trusting one another with the deepest secret of which you can never tell any other soul. Kaithline is the root cause of all of this. She brought a great transformation of my love life. She is the women any man would wish to have. I asked "Dear beloved, lets live by this newly defined term of what a relationship is throughout the course of our affiliation" knowing very well that we would at all times enjoy the fruits that our affiliation provides.

It was in the midst of July when Kaithline texted me thinking I am one of her old friends Thabo, who is a friend of mine whom I met for a short period of time in grade 12. I never gave her any attention as I was too selfish and that is one of my ugly side that no one knows. Communication would occur there and there when one felt bored. I remember this one time on Sunday noon when I asked "Can we chat" she replied "Sure, why not besides I am bored so why not?" In my mind I would think we are only communicating because there is no one else to keep us company.

Months had gone by and I was sharing my poems under the pen name LULU LUMMITOR with every contact I had on my WhatsApp. Many people including Kaithline thought I was sending chain messages, I know this as Kaithline asked "This Lulu of yours is your role model" (giggles).., she does not trust that I could write such good poems, to a point she thought LULU was a professional poet. As I told her more about the poet she became speechless, never believed I could write such.

Days had gone by and it is the 13th of November 2016 during the night as I continued sharing my poems. The next morning out of amazement, she asked me to write about her…. "I don't know you, so how can I write about you" I said, then she replied" but a picture tells more than thousands of words, so I am pretty sure you can write by just looking at me" I waited for almost an hour and then boom a picture is sent. I admired her beauty, complimented her to the last degree and I fell for her instantly. She thought that was a poem but I stopped her from that thought as I told her the mother nature of my compliments that they are matters of the heart. I asked for her hand and she became tense and walked away. I thought I had pushed her away but she had gone out of her comfort zone and thought about the conditions of my heart.

The next day, the way she was so curious about who I am, I knew she had accepted my feelings for her and she was willing to give me a chance to be with her. One would say that the root of my feelings was because of covetousness as I fell for her beauty. I broke the number one rule of my love life that is „Take time to know her and not rush things". Though as I look back I don't regret, my love for her has grown tall. My heart experienced no pain at all as I was happily in love. I wish the promise we made to each other will become true as what lives within my temperament is real and has no bounds. The day my heart stops beating for her is the day I would not be able to see the heaven skies and walk on this Earth.

There are some people we call friends though we never have a chance to see or touch them. These are the people we find ourselves connected to simply by having one or two things in common. That was the case when I met two crazy friends Thimothy Madixa and Moshe Nthibo on social networks. Everything went accordingly and memories were created, had our ups and downs there and there but still remained firm on our connection.

We would introduce our loved ones to each other and gave ourselves advices when needed. We laughed at our jokes non-stop and in the end we became attached to each other. Sadness was forgotten within me as my life was filled with nothing but joy. Times got hard as Moshe in just a blink of a moment lost his sister, I thought that was the end of a happy soul in him. Despite the grief he was facing, he still made me laugh and I wondered where he found the strength and courage from. He told me about all of the incredible moments he had with his sister and the fact that she was always happy having him around as he made sure she smiles at all times. Even though I felt like I could go and be there for him physically I made sure he never lost hope and that he should continue going strong.

Weeks had gone by and I am experiencing challenges in my life and felt repentant. I went into an ultimate prayer and started pleading with God to remove enemies and those who look down at me with an evil eye. Out of nowhere, I began losing my friends and those I thought where soul mates. I thought to myself that I was guilty of something that might have caused my loved ones to walk away. It had been days and I forgot about that powerful prayer I made. One day in the midst of the night, God visited me and said "Your prayers have all been answered" I then realized it was God's doings. I had been saved once again from harm. I realized that the saying
"Nothing lasts forever" with these two friends of mine I thought was a plain lie.

The connection was so real or so I thought to myself. I still couldn't get out of the idea of how it all ended; everything happened so quickly but here I am trying to get around that idea. People change and they don't always change into being better people. Timothy chose to sideline my emotions in order to satisfy his other friends. I endured heartache because of him and so I thought I was not his friend whilst I saw him as a friend.

As for Moshe I guess growing a year older changed his thoughts about me, I was never seen as a friend any longer but as a little kid.

His words really caused damage as he said "I don't mingle with kids I am old as I'm old enough to be your uncle". The age difference didn't matter to me as I thought he was my friend but that was not the case for him.

I really fail to come to conclusions whether I should continue calling them friend's or not after such occurrences. Would i still rejoice and feel at ease because they are within my surrounding? Surely I don't know how to feel anymore. He that I used to call a friend has brought shame and heartache that of which I don't think I was going to get past. I expected him to be a shield that would protect me from harm, but instead he turned his back on me when the ecosphere spun over me. A friend became one of those I call enemies and the look on his face was not pleasant at all. He failed to shield me from the universe but that never brought sadness to my life.

I felt no pain from the global entities as I always knew they wanted to see me at my lowest. Looking at my friend along those groups of people brought a great heartache as I was left all alone without a shoulder to lean on. His eyes were so dark red suggesting nothing but evil intentions. He sold himself to the devil and I hoped and wished that he would get out of that fish net. In my thoughts I assumed the devil and death were interconnected, in a sense that they bring heartache. This co-operation of the devil and death remains to be the worst enemy I fear. My life is no longer that of a happy soul but has now been turned to the opposite.

Everyone who is dearest to my heart is taken away from me, leaving my soul wounded forever. A family with no conscious at all, the root cause of their happiness is at the expense of other people's misery.

Every human being cries because of them and instead of feeling sorry at that juncture, they go on further eradicating more souls.

I believe many souls have shed so many tears and indulged in so much melancholy, by now death along with the devil should understand and spare us more strain.

The actions portrayed by this correlation are not at all pleasing to our lives. If only we knew their real roots we would go out of our comfort zone and try to exterminate them. Sometimes I wonder whether God is related to them - in a sense that every time death occurs, people would say the deceased is now living in a better environment with his creator along with his angels.

Dreams are there to show you the way. This is a quote I took from one of the boys I always listen to whenever I am in love since my early stages of childhood. I never knew why I was so glued to it in a sense that some words along the song I couldn't recite. There must be a story behind this occurrence but at that moment I never thought of it this way. I seem to think for what tomorrow will bring and how I would achieve the challenges of tomorrow. Now that I think of it, the dreams I had about my late grandfather which became true I now know that dreams really are there to show you the way. Though I am a visionary person I fail to understand why I couldn't see it coming, the death of my aunties.

Upon my arrival at home after having written my final grade 10 paper, I saw my mom's car parked outside our home. That was unusual and I felt my world shaking as I knew something was wrong. I opened the door, stood at the door step and asked "mom, why are you back so early" she replied with a white lie that she has a headache. I could see it was more than that and I became honest with her as I wanted to know what is troubling her.

She said death occurred at home, my heart pumped million miles in a split of a second and I asked "who had been promoted into another world" she said: "aunty is no more".

At that juncture, I thought about how my uncle far away from us, on his birthday finding out about such how was he coping. I thought I could call him but he was way too far to be reached. A mother left behind two boys, one being too young to experience such. My other aunty was still in her hometown Transkei and failed to make it to the funeral.

In less than just a month another tragedy occurred. It all happened in a blink of a second, word got out that she is not feeling well on Friday and Tuesday night her existence on this earth came to an end while lying in a hospital bed. I can still remember everything that happened that night. It was 19h00 when we heard strange sounds on the roof that of which no one knew where it came from. Granny in great anticipation holding a blade said "tsena wena if onyaka gobona gore kemang" meaning enter if you want to see the real me. Then minutes later a phone call came through from the hospital.

My aunty was being asked a lot of questions and she did not know what was wrong and I hurriedly rushed out of the room as my thoughts were focused on the fact that we had lost her. When they asked for an elder she went into the other room and as I walked past, I saw her hand dropping I could see how weak and speechless she was. Then out of tears my aunties closed the door I knew that it was all over.

All I wanted was to be there for my cousins but I was told to be too young to go that night as they were all alone. The next morning I still couldn't believe it and it was the 19th of December. OH, dear Lord will we spend a day of celebration in sadness, I thought to myself with eyes soaked in tears.

I grabbed my phone and called my cousin Leonard and couldn't even say a word, my heart was in great pain and my face was not at all pleasant, he dropped the phone call and I understood his actions.

I took a bath in the early morning, my aunt said: "where are you going" out of shock I said "I am going to check on my cousins".

Guess what happened next, I was told I am not going anywhere because I am too young, even the day of the burial I was restricted to attend the final send off. The only thing on my mind was questions of whether we are too young to say our final goodbyes to our aunty. It seemed unfair to both our aunt and us, sometimes I even wonder how her soul is. Is she resting well? I think her soul is not at all at ease because we never said goodbye to her.

Though she was not the same age as us but I still think there was a strong bond every time she saw us, but this is a situation we cannot change. The only thing we can do is blame the old generation with their strict rules of age as to who is allowed and who is not to attend a funeral. Even now, four years later after her death I still wish I could say my final goodbye just to escape from the cage my heart got locked in all these years since her departure on Earth.

CHAPTER VII

18 December 2016 was truly a day of sadness. I spent the day lying on my resting bed thinking hard. My girlfriend Kaithline failed to do the one thing I asked from her which was taking things to the next level and acknowledging the fact that we were in a relationship to the global entities. Upon agreement I knew it was all a bluff, she just agreed to make me feel good and it seemed real.

By the time it was around 17h00, I was feeling repentant, I grabbed my cellphone and called someone I could talk to. There is no better person than her best friend Florence. We started talking and valid points were made that I am being stubborn and seemed to be insecure though her sayings would enter through one ear and go out to the next. I am way too stubborn because this is what I want and not need.
The roots of this never came out of love but feeling lonely in a relationship. Being ignored to the last degree that I couldn't take it, thus asking for what I know will never happen was the only option. Frustrations ran deep within my temperament as I thought of only two things, either I am just another guy to her or that she has a new boyfriend which she loves way too much or she is ashamed of me. I had already accepted that I've lost her even though she was still mine. Communication was dead. The next morning I sent a poem that is dedicated to a 37 year old lady who lost her twins during seventh month of pregnancy to my entire contact lists on WhatsApp.

My girlfriend Kaithline used the poem as a scapegoat to escape to our agreement. With a sadistic eye, I looked at her actions and played along as she accused me of cheating. I still tried to show her that what she is saying is truly wrong.

Going out of my comfort zone I gave her the numbers of the lady as I had nothing to hide, out of disbelief she asked "what do you expect me to do with her numbers as I never asked for them" I couldn't even reply to her idiotic texts and I knew she didn't want the existence of our relationship. Even though I saw this happening I pretended to be dumb and continued with the flow. I apologized and told her all I was trying to do is to make the lady feel better about what happened to her in the past but was asked if I am the new Dr. Phil?

The argument was truly childish but I managed it pretty well. I pulled out many strings to make her feel better, I thought the argument was because of love, but I was so wrong. I wrote every piece of poetry dedicated to her in hopes that her soul will be restored. During late hours I decide to go have some Litchis as I was really craving for them. At that moment I am thinking of a great story of what chapter seven will all be about as I was completely blank. As I got them my friend from the neighboring house called me for a talk after looking at the pot. Giggles… I asked "what are you preparing?" he said: just a small meal for the family. The conversation was really sweet and we started talking about school and got to know that during high school days we did the same subjects.

As I left I walked to the gate as I wanted to be alone because my girlfriend was really giving me a hard time. I asked my cousin for permission on writing about a sensitive saga that transpired once in his life. The response was indirect but I knew the answer was NO. As I was still enjoying my litchis whilst I was busy writing a piece of a poem a litchi slid through my esophagus and stuck on my throat, I tried to cough it out but it had already gone in too deep. I had begun to choke and I tried by all means to cough out the litchi but I failed. I am now running out of breath and I thought of my grand mom but she was way too far. I tried to scream for help but no voice came out. My eyes wide open I struggled and hit my throat hard and it moved slowly and I managed to cough it out.

I ran around the house out of shock, I guess adrenaline really got to me. I threw the litchi as I saw it as nothing but evil, for it could have taken me out of this Earth in just a blink of a second. My brother without realizing what was wrong as he went out to buy airtime, he told me what I wanted to hear the most but I heard nothing at all. The only thing on my mind was what could have been one of the thousands ways to die. My body was shivering and I ran into my grand mom's chamber, head straight into her pillow and soaked it with my tears. My brother couldn't understand but I never spoke to him because he would run to granny to tell her before I could.

I am thinking of my brother as he was heading towards the gate, the only thing that was on my mind was the litchis and him. OH no! He could have taken them as they looked so red and were to die for. I quickly ran to the gate and he is gone and so are the litchis. I had already portrayed them as evil thus I never wanted my brother to be equipped by them, so I ran down the road trying to stop him but he had already finished them and was on his way back home. As I told him about the incident, he thought I was insane and as we walked together back home with someone within our street I walked forward as my battery was dying and I was telling my girlfriend about the incident. I never looked back as I was in a rush and then out of a blue the guy within our streets passed me by and my brother was nowhere to be seen.

I looked sideways and he was not there, the adrenaline rushed back in as I thought something might have happened to him. I moved up and down at the corners of the street to see if he had not taken a different direction, but he was nowhere to be found, I went down the street and got him on his way back with a lady friend. As we walked home we discussed issues of discomfort and laughed as they sound crazy and stupid. Upon arrival at home I charged my phone and continued talking to my girl, talking about the incident of the litchi.

I texted "I nearly died today", to my surprise, I got one of the worst unfriendly replies which read "owk" and I couldn't believe what my eyes just read but my heart broke into a million of pieces, my eyes on the other hand glittered with tears as I realized my presence meant nothing in she whom I thought wanted nothing less than a life with me.

What could have been the end of my existence on this earth is "owk" to the one I seem to be sharing a heart with.

By virtue of that comment, I knew I was simply wasting my time in the relationship, the happiness I thought existed came to an end and I eventually stopped caring. My heart got filled with nothing but emotions of anger and evil. The only wish in my mind at that time was to meet her just to look at her so I could spit saliva in her face. I would be doing this in order to just alert her that she is nothing but a disgusting creature on this Earth. A heart is not a trash bin meant for collecting all the rubbish of the world but a golden pot meant for collecting nothing but memories of this Earth. However, the one I once called a friend, a sister and most importantly the one I thought I would marry saw me as nothing but a rubbish bin.
I wonder why she said all those hurtful words, but I don't think I would be able to communicate with her after such. I guess even though I never told her that I wanted nothing to do with her, we both knew that our existence in each other's lives was futile and there was no way we could ever kiss and make up. All I could do was to think whether there was any soul out there whose heart would be shattered if I had died. Life along with its challenges for me is truly unbearable, no soul as young as me should indulge in such pain. I guess I am still here simply because God never left my side, I survived what could have been one of the thousand ways to die. The next morning I could still feel the litchi right by my throat blocking every valve of breath, I surrendered everything and thanked God for most his amazing.

With his protection I could still see the sun shining right through my window and hear the cooing sounds of the birds and not forgetting the great melody tunes of the cicadas.

By 9h00 I prepared a good feisty meal as I got ready for the moment I've been waiting for, that being getting my drivers learner's qualification. Surprisingly before I got there the craziest moment of my life occurred. As I was 3 kilometers away from the destination I saw a taxi and I thought to myself that the taxi fare would be as little as it is not far away. Giggling… I asked "how much would it cost me from this destination to the traffic department?" the taxi driver responded "it would cost you the normal price which is R10" I got surprised and said it's fine I will continue walking as I don't have that amount of cash. Surprisingly, the taxi driver was Mishack, who grew up with my cousin Leonard and he offered me a free lift. Inside the taxi I was asked why I was behaving like that and got knowledge that the taxi driver took care of me during my primary school days, however I didn't recall anything about him. He took me down the memory lane and I got the knowledge of who he was and remembered the old times I endured around him.

Memories were created in just five minutes and already I had arrived at my destination. As I filled the forms I thought it would be one of the easiest tasks ever but that was just a thought in my mind. As I went for an eye test I sat before the eye test machine and started stumbling upon my feet as the test was seconds away from commencing. I failed the test the first time and my heart was already in discomfort. The pain I endured watching the next person after me getting it right was truly unbearable. I watched him leave the room with a smile on his face without looking back. I pleaded with the officer to give me a second chance, but the outcome was the same even though I thought I got everything right. He referred me to an Optometrist as he denied me one final chance to go through the eye test which would qualify me to the second last step before I can write my learner's driver test.

I felt bad and thought all my plans would be derailed and that I would be restricted to write my drivers learners as I am visually impaired.

I walked back home with sadness in my eyes and called mom to alert her that I have eye problems. She told me it is a genetic problem that everybody at home has and told me she would get me spectacles.

Upon my arrival at home the worst is yet to happen. I knew nothing of airtime missing but my grandmother was certain that I took it before I left. Out of voluminous number of people at home I got blamed because I was the only one in the house when she put her phone on the charger. I failed to understand why I was blamed because the airtime could have been used during my absence at home. I got furious because of the accusations taking into consideration how my day went at the traffic department.

Nobody tried to calm me down as I portrayed my dark side. I was so furious because they accused me of something I had no knowledge of. Anyone who was in the house could have used the airtime without her knowledge during my absence. Though I am used as a scapegoat simply because I went out of home suggesting that I was running away after taking what was not mine while they knew I had errands to run by going to the traffic department. The pain that I felt was truly excruciating. To make matters worse granny never believed me. I said a few wrong words that I shouldn't have said leaving her soul shattered into pieces.
I was certain that I was leaving home that night, I just couldn't be in a place whereby I am used as a scapegoat whenever things don't go accordingly. A house that once I called home would be a house filled with strangers as they cannot be trusted.

The gate was locked, but as I tried to jump the fence, my brother Austin pleaded with me to calm down and reassess the situation.

He was there for me but I pretended as if I never heard a word he said. He never gave up on me and still spoke words that sat well with my soul.

As I rushed back into the house fetching keys to unlock the gate he said "its fine if you leaving but the least you can do is to tell me where you going to, so that I can go with you" I surrendered and went into my slumbering chamber to cool off. I was too ashamed to look at everyone's eye in the family as I they had seen a monster in me.

I wondered if they would continue to smile with me after what I proved to be in their faces. Wicked spirits haunted me and I was too afraid to be around people. My grandmother had been shattered by the words I rendered. She picked up a phone and called my mom to alert her of my anger as she couldn't take it. My mom knows me better than anyone else and she managed to calm me down and bring a smile to my face. The saying that goes "nobody knows a child better than a mom" became real by virtue of talking to her.

I was able to face the tunes of my music, though mom pointed out factors to me why I ought to apologize but I failed to put words of sorry where they were due. Mom along with granny might have thought that there was no heart in me for them and that I told myself tales that granny deserved every little thing I said simply because she was wrong. I truly didn't believe there was any person feeling the same pain I was enduring. The pain I felt seeing granny's face was excruciating. She still tried to be the strong women she has always been, but through her eyes and gestures I could see deep within her. Seeing her like that affected me heavily as I knew I was the reason behind her broken heart.

The one grandchild whom she expected nothing but tender, love and care broke it all off.

All I could think of was her high blood pressure, my blood boiled in great fear that something bad might happen to her. My fear came into reality ten minutes after she went into her slumbering chamber.

As I was visiting my own chamber she started coughing, I rushed into her room and she coughed to the greatest extent that I couldn't bear the sound of it. Instead of helping, I ran out of the house into the corner so that I don't the unbearable sound of her cough. My emotions have been pushed to its highest-peeks and I couldn't hold myself but cry. I went into yet another ultimate prayer to GOD and GRANDFATHER to put all measures in place to help her heal.

Unbearable thoughts in my mind as to why a child has to go through such pain were in the center of my mind. I was too scared to go back inside the house simply because of fear of the bad that might happen to my grandmother. Daily I am restless on my own bed, I don't know how to enjoy a beauty sleep because I would always be awakened by Grandma's painful cough. All those thoughts in my mind strengthened me and I realized that granny was the center of my life and the only reason why I was living on this Earth. Minutes later I went back to the house and head straight into her room and asked "can I prepare warm water for you so that the coughing would stop?" She looked at me and glanced with a reply "yes please" she felt loved and realized though I was angry at her the love I had for her never died. In a blink I prepared her warm water and that night I slept peacefully simply because she never coughed throughout the night and soul was at ease.

CHAPTER VIII

Definitely when I want to describe this fair creature, I just get tongue tied whenever I wish to recite words of the heart. It's like there seems to be no amount of lyrics or verses to be orated that could sum up how emotional I tend to be when her appellation is called or visits my heart. When we first met I thought to myself that she was just one of the lassies whom are just a fair creature of an epoch. Without knowing, without the knowledge to comprehend things clearly I didn't see it coming, it hit me with a surprise that my heart would only be in need of her alone. I never knew that the very same girl Jolie would be the only girl whom my heart would rhythm in lieu of.

Compliments of all sorts would fly around like butterflies. The beauty that she was blessed with from all heaven skies, the smile that subsists truncated in her internal fragment, in great anticipations my only desire was to be with her so I could perceive her blessings every minute of my life. My heart felt completely strange, the greatness of my feelings for the lady was completely different from feelings that I had for my past lassies.

I knew that my love for her would exist for a lifetime as when I thought of her physiognomies my eyes drenched of tears of joy advocating the extent of the joy she brought in my life. Furthermore nothing was strong enough to break this feeling I had about that lady, only death was strong enough to alert us, but despite that we would live each day smiling and creating golden memories heading towards the future.

In just a few months everything changed into the worst. Death never occurred but what used to be was extinct.

I seemed puzzled as to why all of my relationships failed, but who am I to question the Lord Judge for my life, He planned it and He knew what He was doing- all I have to do is appreciate and accept whoever I am. Even though I tried to comprehend my life in the best way I can, I still failed to reach conclusions of who I was. In my own understanding and introspecting myself to an extent I see myself as an outsider in the Earth as no one truly understands how I am. Even though I am human just like everyone else I am crucified on facets I have no control of. I cannot get out of the notion that I am an adjudicated ambiance. Ever since I was a pre-school student I loved a women that I thought I truly loved and even now more than six years later I still wish I can have just two minutes to tell the matters of the heart. To God I cried, trying to heal in the hands of my soul reviver because a fair creature of an epoch is a stumbling block to my emotional state of my sentiment. Whenever I think of that lassie all I do is shed a tear that flows down from my cheeks because I have been deprived of a chance to express my feelings.

Taking everything nine years ago whereby nothing but golden memories were created in different places such as the room filled with soul buddies club members, sharing a meal during lunch time and sitting next to each other in that massive hall waiting for our merits of excellence. In all my living years way back I played a major role in her life along with her brother. I reflect upon my life as being a twofold situation due to thinking for myself and Brie, the thought that was in my mind was that we are soul mates and maybe just maybe we would be together in the near future.

To my surprise it appears that the idea I had about her was a fib the entire time, it had not been about ripeness but a choice to snub. I wish I never invested so much in her to a point that I was two in one in a sense that she was part of my life, perhaps maybe I would be able to say goodbye but it's not easy even though she was never physically there but she was emotionally there all along.

What made me uncertain about her true feelings was the fact that she always glanced at me with one of the warmest smile I could ever get and I loved every moment of the feelings that were in play. I guess I forgot the saying that a book should not be judged by its cover or the fact that a beautiful fruit might contain a worm. Deep within she was not the same as how her physical appearance portrayed her to be. I guess the smile she waved at me was just a flute and maybe she saw something funny about me that she laughed silently and all I could see was a smile. She judged me silently and that alone made me feel misplaced, tormented and most importantly judged on characteristics beyond my control.

As I try to think about it, I am left in arrears trying to find out the cause of such hatred. All my plans to get her to be in the same room as me failed. The greatest wish I have is to simply be honored with a chance to utter the conditions of my heart so that she can finally notice that while I was a diamond in her eyes all along she was too blind to see the light offered by my presence in her life.

I truly deserved better than what she offered. Way back I used to be the king of happiness but now I seem to be living in a lion's den, because in the future I know I will get wounded. My soul drips dark red blood while my veins and arteries are failing my respiratory system causing damage to each and every organ in my body. My favorite anthem was to love her forever. Everything that I shared was out of the goodness of my heart. I told the truth at all times about the feelings that lied within my temperament but the ambiance disappointed me. She disguised herself in the prettiest smile and out of stupidity I fell for her charm. It was hilarious because the charm was only a disguise and I thought that we were all rejoicing for good reasons, to my surprise, the feelings were not mutual at all. A promised milky and world of sweetness, in just a minute became a universe filled with bitterness. I guess it was time to grow and move on with life.

I know for a fact that deep within me, there is a special seed that waits to germinate. It matters not who I think I am or the environment which I live in. I am not defined by materialistic possessions that surround me but circumstances that are detrimental to my wellbeing. The heartaches I have come across in the past are nothing but just lessons on my long walk to success. Even if the obstacles seems too hard to conquer, no matter how hard I fall to the ground, I will never lose hope because I know time, days, weeks, months and years won't be the same. Despite being heartbroken several times, it doesn't mean I don't deserve to be loved, but it is shaping me into being a better partner when tomorrow comes. Life does not remain constant due to being disappointed at some point in life. Somewhere across the world, bigger thing awaits me that will be mine forever.

Nobody is perfect which is why we fail to overcome certain challenges. Certainly, failing is just a hindrance but it does not stop me from being someone worthwhile in life. We live at times whereby our greatest desire is to see the people from our surroundings happy while we forget about our own happiness. Peer pressure is an everyday LIFE EVENT that serves as stumbling block to our future plans. Allowing temptations from the utterings of our friends is the same as acknowledging that what you desire and wish to be takes second preference in comparison with your friends. This was the case for me on the 22nd of November 2016 after writing my English paper of my final lap in school. As I try to think of all the activities that occurred that day, I totally become bitter and disgusted to the level of stupidity I dragged myself into.

As the clock reached midday, friends and some classmate decided to go out to celebrate their last paper. Having no backbone is a serious issue and after many preaching of the same verse by my folks I only realized it this very moment. I had not finished writing my exams but I decided to go out with friends to consume vast amounts of alcohol.

The worst part about all this gathering was that people had a reason to celebrate and I never had one, I was simply a follower and they were my leaders.

We drank vast amounts of liquid and I still fail to understand how I could do such. Drinking alcohol is not a sin, but drinking excessively is the problem because it would only make you act irrational. I drank to a certain point that I slept off the park like it was midnight forty winks. My legs were too weak to walk kilometers to my house. "What am I going to do" I asked Alex with fear of how my mom will react when she sees me in that state.

Many people might say I acted out of stupidity, but the pain that I felt at that time was unbearable. It was never out of disrespect when I called my mom to fetch me. I did so because I knew I wouldn't make it home alive if I decided to walk. Choices are made daily; I had to make a choice not that of which will satisfy me, but also people around me.

I had to make a choice concerning my existence on earth, had to choose to either disappoint mama or try to make myself the shining star. In the end, had I tried to be a shining star I would probably be hit by a car. Afraid of death, pained by the trauma that mommy would go through if I had died. As she answered the phone, I could tell by her shrilling voice, "You drank alcohol", I tried to deny it but my voice did sound different. As she arrived at the garage, she realized that I was indeed drunk and all I saw rolling down her cheeks was tears of disappointment. She tried to contain the pain all by herself but she failed. She then decided to bring in a third party to the equation, my uncle who is my role model and someone who sees only perfection in me.

I had to face the tune of the melody I had started and it was never a good sight. The worst would then follow afterwards.

I was told to pack my bags and go home the day after my final exam. I thought to myself that it was just a moment of frustration and that it would change. The very same day I was ordered to go home is the very same day of which I planned to meet my girlfriend Kaithline.

The thought of experiencing the proposed consequences of my actions was truly unbearable. How can I be stripped off what would become one of the greatest memories of my life? There were so many answered questions in my mind, so i tried to overcome the impossible. It was Monday morning, between 00:00 and 01:00 when I decided to make a phone call to Kaithline as we planned to meet the following day. However, with the new proposed events that I had to go home I tried asking her to come that same Monday. I could feel the pressure I put her through but I did all that out of love because seeing her would make me happy. She ended up dropping the phone call because the conversation was unbearable for lovers. I lay awake on my bed thinking of circumstances I had no control of. As time approached 03:00, my phone rang and it was none the other than the one who was on my mind, Kaithline.

A heartfelt expression was made and I couldn't help but shed more tears. She promised that she would be able to come and see me. I was over the moon as my loved one would be the last face I would see before I went home for the remaining days of the year.
Just like other days, happiness turned into heartache. As I was in that exam room, what kept me going was how special that day would be. Even now I can never tell, whether it was a lie or it was nothing but the truth that the taxi couldn't get the required people to leave Siyabuswa to Middelburg.

The time was 16:00 and all I did was think of her safety. Thus I told her to go home, her safety was the first priority for me. I would rather not see her for one day than to live forever without seeing her because of being impatient to the point that safety came last.

Even though I could share my sentiments with her, I was broken to the core. To make matters worse, I would sleep with a broken heart and wake up to my misery only for petrol to be added on my problems. I was so angry that morning. I was supposed to be resting but I was awakened to get ready to vacate the house.

I was stopped from going to matric dance for the right reasons. That was one of the greatest upsets I ever encountered. I was ordered to go home immediately after finishing my exams simply because I drank alcohol. I was not the only one who suffered but my loved ones had to experience the pain too. The promises I had made to my loved ones would not come true and this was because of my bad behavior. At that time, all I wanted from my family was to support me, but instead they took away my happiness and that infuriated me.
As my mom left me by the taxi rank, I felt like I could run to a friend's place because I had plans I couldn't miss. Nonetheless I swallowed my pride and went home but I switched off my cellphone because of anger so that they wouldn't reach me. My laundry was dirty, never had time to wash it or at least prepare for the journey. Luckily for me, they never told anyone back home about what I did and so they welcomed me with open arms. For a few hours, I couldn't be myself because I felt rejected by my mom. I couldn't tell if they noticed at home or not that I was so reluctant in communicating with both my mom and my uncle.

They both tried their best to create communication between me and them respectively and that was because their actions were based on love. Nobody understands or feels proud of receiving tough love at that juncture but now looking back at the past I am thankful for the love my family provided me with.

After I realized the above notion, I swallowed my pride and asked for forgiveness from Mom and Uncle Freddie on my recent bad behavior and they forgave me.

The fun memories I endured with my siblings at home made me forget everything and I never felt sorry for myself on how my arrival back home came about.

My cousin Charles who had recently left home on a vacation to Uncle's place at Lephalale had to come back home earlier than he had planned. He had to return back home to sort out the circumstances based on his academic results as the school couldn't release it to anyone except him. As he got his results, his character changed and he never came for a visit at our house. Such behavior out of him sat uncomfortably with grand mom and she questioned us about his recent behavior and she asked us to go look for him to ascertain if he is okay or not.

Something clicked in my mind, before he even went to Lephalale, I had a dream of him pulling that stunt. It made sense and I was the only one who could find him. During the day, we searched for him without any luck along with my brothers. Disappointed that we never found him, we returned back home. As the night approached, I left home to his place again in hopes that I would find him. His room is in the backyard thus his presence or absence remained unnoticed. I knocked on his door without any signal that he was indeed in the room. As I was about to leave, my instincts would not let me. I knew he was in the room and in order to prove my assumptions I had to find the spare key to that room. As I tried to open the door, the key wouldn't go in because he had locked with a key from inside the room. As he opened the door, I thanked all heaven skies that he was okay but you could tell by just looking at him that he was not himself at all. The room was a mess, I could smell alcohol and some smoke suggesting that he was smoking. I never entertained it much, because I knew the pain he felt in his heart. Absolutely, there was no way he could enjoy my presence in that room. I had to be strong for him so he could feel accepted and be assured that someone out there still cared about him.

We went out for a few drinks, the purpose of such was to forget about all the obstacles we were facing. Things went smooth and as we were walking back to his house, there was a car standing still by the bridge and everyone seemed relaxed there, thus, we stood still without a cause, well that was the thought in my mind, I said "Charlie, let's take another route back home", terrified by such as we took another route thinking that the car would have moved already.

To our surprise the car was stuck, and the driver was a guy we knew, we were delighted by that, as fear was completely erased. At the end of the day my vision was achieved and I was more than just gratified that I brought sunshine in the dark when my cousin was down.

CHAPTER IX

It was Christmas day when I woke up to a wonderful surprise. My uncle had stepped foot in the kitchen preparing breakfast specially dedicated to the grandchildren. That moment I was due to go to be with my older uncle in the driving grounds as I was being taught how to drive. I guess I am too different from every child, what the elders would say is that I behave in a manner of which resembles the white regime. I know I am an emotional person and I still ate the breakfast prepared by my uncle. To me it was more than just breakfast, but nobody understood. As the day unfolded, the boys took off to go celebrate the day, but their joy would only last for a few hours. The clock reached 18:00 noon, I knew that they consumed alcohol and the rest of the family was looking for them (Charles, Austin and Melvin). I had to find them before anyone else did to warn them about what was going to happen. I couldn't believe my eyes when I found them as they couldn't even walk straight because of the vast amount of alcohol they consumed.

As their older brother, I advised them to use the backyard because the family was sitting at the front of the house. I prayed hard that they don't realize what had transpired during the day. I knew for sure that if Uncle Freddie found out, it would not end well. I never played my part too, the gates had not been locked yet. What I failed to understand was how Austin got up and vacated the house without my knowledge. While I was in the dining room writing my novel, my uncle came across Austin in the kitchen and noticed some irrational behavior out of him and realized that he was drunk. The tough love he gave them, it truly left me shattered. I tried to tell him to stop because they are too young for that but he failed to listen.

After some time, my mom realized the agony deep within the kids, so she called Uncle Freddy aside to talk to him.

The way things turned out that night was truly horrific for the young boys. Expected to validate their reasons for indulging in such activities, their voices are unheard but their grievance. I went to the room to try to comfort them.

Austin was in so much pain that I couldn't bear it, the tears that flowed through his cheeks was mixed with blood. I got the reason why they indulged in such activities during the day. Certainly, it was to relieve stress on the information they shared amongst the three of them. Circumstances that are detrimental to their wellbeing were discussed and so they confided in alcohol. I couldn't take it when Austin said "They can ask us to answer for our actions but I pray that they don't ask Charles because he was at his lowest". I realized the seriousness of the situation and all I could do was watch the room get flooded by the tears flowing out of my brother's eyes. Anthony, the younger brother after Austin denounced, "brother, I know you might think I care less since I am not shedding any tears like Austin, yet I am hurt by our actions and if we could turn back the hands of time, we would certainly have acted differently."

I had to be a bigger brother by talking to our difficult uncle on going easy on my younger brothers. I managed to talk him out of the thought of emotionally punishing the kids.
The next day and the other days that went by until the last day of 2016 was truly splendid. Everyone was doing an activity at home in preparation for the upcoming year, women where in the kitchen preparing a marvelous cake to celebrate the New Year's season whilst men were cleaning the yard. The year ended at a high note though we came across certain obstacles but we managed to overcome them.

The approach of the New Year was sweet, yet I was tense as I thought of my judgement day. The thought of receiving my Matric results to a disappointment of not making it was my greatest fear ever because I had failed more than just enough and matric pass was the break I was in need of.

Deep down, I knew that I passed but was not certain on which symbol I passed with. Before I realized it, I was already waiting for few hours to receive that result statement. Emotionally and physically traumatized by stress, I never knew where to touch and hold as I was jumpy. My worst fear was erased but not completely. As I got proof for my hard work, I got the knowledge that I passed but not according to my level of expectation. Nonetheless, the support of the family got me going. Even though I was stressed on the outcome of my results, I had to be grateful that I made it. I realized that some of my friends and other classmates would actually celebrate being in my shoes in comparison to what they were feeling for not making it. Sometimes we will see ourselves as failures in life while other people see us as those who have succeeded in life.

Time to leave everything behind and get around the fact that I am now a man embarking on the world of adults. MAMA won't be around to spoon feed me nor clean after me as I am due to stand on my own by implementing what my family taught me during my childhood. I embarked on a trip to Turfloop University to acquire for tertiary education. I was not scared at all travelling to an unknown destination because I knew I had God beside me all the time. Arriving at my destination, my cousin's girlfriend, Melda made me feel at home as we waited for Chris and so I felt safe under the new surroundings. The next day was nothing but a stress, pain and greatest disappointment in my life. My results on the other hand was not pleasing at all compared to other freshmen. Authorities of the institution were not at all supportive but turned a blind eye on an oppressed soul thriving for a better future.

I tried by all means to change the situation but circumstances didn't favor me at all. Through thick and thin, I went out of my way to try to get the education I deserve. Thursday morning, I rushed to the premises early in the morning thinking circumstances would change, only to meet a precious young soul titled Fiesta.

At that juncture, after enduring much sweat I accepted my fate that I would never be in UL (UNIVERSITY OF LIMPOPO). I got to realize that sometimes we think of going to a certain destination for certain reasons, but the outcome is not always as we expect it to be. God is at all times providing his mercy in his own way, sometimes the gifts that we are entitled to are miles away from us. When the time is right for acquiring what God has put in place for us, he will direct us to that destination himself. Though I was never qualified to learn under such premises, I never gave up in life. The single thought in my mind was "God guides me in paths of righteousness for his name's sake". Furthermore goodness and love will follow me all the days of my life, and I will dwell in the house of the LORD forever.

Time elapsed and I found myself with my luggage preparing to leave Turfloop with my Uncle. Indeed, it was a great trip but it had to end soon. I was pained by thoughts that I was seen as a weakling, since I got insufficient credits to get accepted by any Tertiary institution. As we were on our way back home, my uncle advised me on how to conduct myself throughout the aftermath of what I encountered at Turfloop. I heard each and every word he rendered and I became stronger than a lion, more vicious to receive the best education ever. I gained emotional, physical and spiritual intelligence through words that came out of Uncle Freddie. I had a vision from that period onwards. My mind seemed to have reached its limits. All that existed was thoughts of how tomorrow would be like, be it that I make amends by changing circumstances that surrounded me or not, it all lied within me and nobody else.

We call days that had already elapsed the past simply because it is fixed and will remain like that forever. Yet, we call tomorrow the future due to having an opportunity to make better informed choices that of which will prosper in the long run. Failure is not my weakness, but my strength to see clearly what I did wrong and what needs to be changed so that I get different results.

Change is good when you know what your goals are and I know what my goals are thus change is required. Sensational Lummitor's thoughts is to sleep, think, create opportunities, be goal driven and work towards the desired goal in the best way I possibly can. I realized that life is not easy come, easy go but all about the hardships of a human being's existence. Rules of living preordain that I acknowledge my mistakes, correcting them is my only desire. I ought to be a new soul, better son, better friend, better brother and a better person. My emotional state of mind tortured by voluminous number of people it's all in the past, my motive is greed and desire to change my past into a better future.

As the story unfolds, connection between binary ambiances Karise and I was established. I felt like I was in another world because daily we exchanged sweet communications in attempt to establish a special seed broken in half which is planted in both souls. Miles away from each other, a lassie situated in Pretoria while I was still in Middelburg. I do believe that God's magnificent touch is amazing, he moved me away from my mom to meters away from Karise's place of learning. I felt special, was truly blessed with her presence in my life. I left my loved one Pride, because she is the one I completely fell in love with. The thought that I am now meters away from my new love and the idea that I'm kilometers" away from the one who shares a heart with me led me to make stupid choices. At that time it felt all sweet, yet I had not declared my vows to my new love. I recall such as the stupidest mistake of my life as I was seen as a mere friend and nothing more.

Though I was not aware of such circumstances till one fair Sunday whereby she invited me to church. Last minute invite, I dropped everything and prepared myself for the wonderful trip to see the one my heart beats for yet she didn't know.

I can't recall if she told me the truth or not when she said she couldn't come to church rather, I ought to visit her. The funny part was I got such information after hours of my arrival.

Wondered around the streets of Thembisa Centre with grieve of not meeting my love. Met in the streets, offered me a hug I couldn't return because I was love struck by her beauty. I truly didn't believe my eyes and it was all nice up until my departure time arrived. At that time, I was comfortable and I was ready to hold her in my arms, unfortunately she was not keen on doing such anymore and reason for that I didn't know. I felt bad about that, but I thought it meant nothing at all just a simple game. What I never realized was the feelings or care she had for me changed after realizing my true natural appearance. A phone call to report on the safe journey I had rang but remained unanswered. I could understand from that moment that I was never cared for by the one whom serves as the queen of my heart. What a painful story of my life, rejected because of being different to how she perceived me.

Circumstances seemed to be failing my heart as each second of my life was lived with the thought that I was losing benedictions that existed within Karise. Looks can deceive I acknowledge and that is an undeniable fact we can't hide in this life. Being rejected should not serve as a disadvantage in any human being's life, but should actually be an advantage to our wellbeing because of one reason only and that is the fact that we are appreciated enough to be saved from the trauma we would experience if our vows to that person were accepted.

A two-faced scenario is that sometimes the truth is denied to be a lie and vice-versa and that is one of the reasons why I couldn't forget easily about Karise.

Loving her gave me courage and reason to live, a smile existing on my beautiful face rests in the presence of Karise's availability in my life. Even though life was sweet, I made a terrible mistake by focusing too much on the present and forgot about everything that existed in my life.
I thought my life was complete and that alone was one of the worst mistakes I ever experienced. Being happy is not a promise that things will remain the same forever, but I was too stubborn to realize that. Out of disbelief, the deeds performed right in my presence were so unbearable to watch. It was so painful to see your loved one sharing expressions from the heart to another man who absolutely doesn't deserve her. Yet alone, it was so painful for me to witness such, because I knew no man in this earth would appreciate her as much as I do. I always rendered a speech to her which read "nobody will love you better than me and everyone who you meet trying to share a life with you will disappoint you." I rendered those words because I acknowledged the true feelings that existed deep within my heart and I was aware that in all heaven skies the scenario does exist.

True love comes in many shapes and portrays different outcomes, loving a person whole-heartedly is not a promise that you have met your true love and that is what I realized after being restricted to live upon the feelings existing deep within for this special lassie. Days went by and I had to put a fake smile on my face to fool the world that I am strong yet I failed to fool my heart. I continued to try to mend my heart by trying to show her that I truly love her. Things got out of control in one fair night, when insults from all angles came out of my loved one. Being told that I was a useless being who is only good in writing, yet an academic failure

. I took it like a man but deep down I was broken not to mention the surprise of being showed no love. Another man's heart was satisfied at the expense of my heart.

The following day was miserable and my sister from another mother told me that my loved one's step mom has been remembered in all heaven skies. My mind unable to function I ran out of my class to go to her college to try and give her my support. Unfortunately, she was never there and she wanted nothing from me.

Phone call rang fifty times without any answer, I felt scared thinking the anger she portrayed the other night might have led her to hurting herself. At that juncture I never knew her place of stay thus I couldn't go to look for her in a place I don't know of. Unexpected surprise from the one loved by my loved one, he expressed hearts of the sentiment to another lassie, times of great difficulty from the one who loves him. "This is some sort of witchcraft, how can a person can be so cruel", I asked myself, then I thought to myself again that whatever is planned by all heaven skies we ought to follow otherwise God's wrath will be felt in our entire surroundings. I tried to fix what should have never been broken, but I received no luck in my attempt since it seemed like all heaven skies had closed the chapter of our affiliation. As I left, I promised not to look backwards and I am now more evil hearted than ever. I stopped caring because of the pain that had been inflicted deep within me. Looking at who I seem to be by just perceiving my life as a whole, if I raised my voice truly speaking the universe's mouth would be left hanging out of disbelief. I have to acknowledge that there are many precious diamonds that waits to be under my wing because I am worth it. The only thought in my mind is how blessed and happy I was in the past. Nowadays, thinking about those who brought joy in my life, I get affected in my innermost fragment. This certainly shall not be the end of my existence on this Earth, I will recuperate and be a novel soul, though I was once contented today I am devastated.

Loving a soul is not a problem, it is actually one of the things that builds us in life and enables us to accept the past that of which treated us unkindly. Accepting and moving to a different slope or saga in life is hard but what made it easier for me was knowing that nothing will come alright if I remain fixed at one point. Everything I had built with Karise came to an end and so I had to close that chapter and focus on new aspects as I wait for someone who will appreciate the love I would offer at all times.

When you think about the life you are living on Earth, after reassessing the heartaches that you endure daily, please never think that your existence on this earth is just a mere shame. No matter what life throws at you, always accept the situation and move on. In order to be able to solve challenges, we ought to accept what is being given. The story behind accepting good or bad is that we acknowledge and come to senses of how we can counteract anything we come across in life. Thoughts of negativity such as no one cares about me, I am not worthy of such and such items, ERASE THOSE THOUGHTS COMPLETELY OUT OF YOUR MIND. Uttering negative words in your own mind means that you are not aware and in control of who you have become in life.

At all times when we pray to our Lord, we beg for power and knowledge of who we are and who our real friends are. That ultimate prayer will bring unexpected results. Rejection, betrayal, termination of friendship or relationship might seem to be an aspect of negativity, but upon realization that is what you asked for in your prayer. Never cry because you are rejected or whether your friendship with your loved one came to an end, God is at all times beside you and he never forsakes his children. Give Opportunities Daily (GOD) removes certain people in our lives not because we don't deserve them but because they are not linked to our long term future endeavors but short term endeavors.

That is the knowledge I applied throughout my entire existence but that does not mean I never felt any pain. Truth be told pain turned me into someone I never pictured myself to be, I have become a total monster in disguise, a predator always seizing to clinch his jaws on other souls without shame at all. Heart-break brought about anger deep within my temperament. It existed deep within like a small planted seed that was waiting to germinate.

I pretended as if I was strong to the world but deep down I endured so much pain, at some time I thought dying was the only option. I lied to myself that I would never let anything of discomfort to my wellbeing change me, but it was too late, the seed had already prospered into a plant of anger. I tried getting rid of the pain by soaking my pillow with tears. My body already started to deteriorate due to sleepless nights caused by heartache from my loved one. The pain was too much that I ended up exploding due to the feeling of being over my original being. The abhorrence within me has been unleashed. The titles that I was defined with such as an adorable sweet little child was no longer a true reflection of who I was, all that I seem to be now is a devil disguised in costumes of the angels. My voice possesses so much violence like that of a roaring hungry Lion.

I am not who I used to be simply because of the world's negligence. When they ought to care for me, they turned a blind eye.

Certain things happened without me realizing the damage I was causing due to my uncontrollable anger. The only reason for my existence seems to be nothing than the slaughtering of a young soul's emotions. A young man brutalized his loved one's emotions by acting cheap, at the end he gained nothing but a stab of a knife straight into his heart. Mind completely stuck, failed to choose words to render due to anger. Out of stupidity he lost it all, lost everything he fought for. Rendering the words sorry would never erase the pain felt by the ones who cared for him without expecting anything in return.

It is a fact that expensive material things or millions of the world can never repair the broken sentiment I caused. It costs nothing to appreciate, but for me it felt like giving up my life for someone else whilst death is my worst fear. Broken so many times by the ones I trusted, my little trust was nothing but a complete shame in the eyes of my loved ones.

I find no reason why people should continue loving me because I am just a young man who is out there to cause havoc simply because I have been treated unkind by my loved ones. Love me no more my love, I deserve nothing but events that take place in the house of bad deeds (hell) itself. Restrict the tears from falling down thy cheeks because of a lunatic fringe whose existence is FUTILE on this EARTH. If a child could be exchanged, I would have had thousands of families because I am nothing but a disgrace to human kind. I am just a black sheep born in a wrong family, what a complete disgrace am I to the society!!!

I seem to be a child cursed from birth, a child with no direction in life, at all times walking in the land of the evil. A troubled child deep within seemingly lost since birth by being raised by none of his blood. Rejected by nature, the world never accepted me as a human being worthy enough to be on Earth.

I sometimes think that my presence on Earth was the worst mistake ever done by GOD because I think I belong in hell, where the devil's work is at all times appreciated because I am nothing but a stranger in this world. I remain to be a man with no conscious as I inflict damage in the hearts of my loved ones. I wish everybody could stop loving me and join the sweet world and hate the monster who represents nothing but shame in this beautiful land we live in. I seem to be a monster nowadays and I hate every moment of this new soul I have become. A smile used to be a very dear friend to my wellbeing but currently it seems to be a stranger across the streets and I don't know how to accept him as a friend.

The fury within me drives away many souls I wish to equip in my life and I have to accept that the world transformed me by taking away the name I made for myself as a humble young guy by destroying the special seed within me and sold my name to the devil.

The abhorrence within me makes my life a living hell and I still wish I could undo everything but the past can never be altered yet it can be forgotten by shaping my life into the better only if I take control of what is before me in a thoughtful manner. I have learned a hard lesson that sometimes we as individuals happen to indulge in activities we are not proud of. Furthermore we make decisions without being aware that when tomorrow comes we are the ones who will have to experience the effects. Moreover, we tend to forget that every single thing we embark in this life is a mere lesson of some sort in our imperfect lives. The single question that is left out to be answered is what have we learned from the obstacles we encountered in our lives?

Holding on into the past is being outrageous, because days always progress, there's never been a day that went backwards and that was the motive I applied in my life. The ugly truth about life is the fact that we are reluctant to change because we think what we have today can never be replaced. By carefully assessing life as a whole we always get more than what we expect when tomorrow comes. What I don't understand is the fact that we allow ourselves to be draped under the cloud even though we are aware that there is sunshine outside.

I think it's simply because we think crying and complaining about life will somehow ease up the excruciating pain deep within our temperaments. The painful truth that we are unaware of is that we tend to think that holding on into the past will bring about a change in the circumstances currently being faced but it actually breaks us instead of building us into improved souls.

Finally, I had to close the chapter of my association with Karise, I had to acknowledge that I made a mistake by mistaking the joys of our associations to be forever when it was just an ecstasy of an hour. Dust to dust, ashes to ashes, fun of today ends today and just as tomorrow is a new day, it also amounts to new beginnings.

I had to move on towards a better tomorrow and make amends to enable myself to have joy in my life again. The things that happened yesterday will all be erased by what happens today and tomorrow.

After I had closed all doors with Karise, God's grace draped my life and brought Gina to pick up the broken pieces and bring about joy in my life. It was all sweet, I supported her through every obstacle and I believed that she was the last love sub-division even though she was miles away from me, but the love was real. Karise and I still met but the feelings were not mutual and I was too blind to notice. On a fair day I realized that Karise is a black sheep covered with angelic cloth, all I thought at the beginning was that she was an angel, until she did the unthinkable. Gina and I were so in love that we thought nobody could ever take away what we felt for each other. One day as Karise and I met, she practically forced me to take pictures with her and out of stupidity I granted her request.

Later on she would send the pictures to my love to cause havoc. Things got out of control as I had to protect my love but I ended up hurting the one that my heart loves to satisfy the one my mind desires. Even though I realized that I was wrong to tear my soul mate apart, I never acted responsibly because of pride. How can I even delineate the conditions of my heart, I am stuck up in this empty room without a direction of where to from now. I am indulging in an ultimate prayer with the thought that things will prosper between me and my soul mate. I am pained deep within and I am in arrears trying to mend the heart that I broke to please outsiders.

The organ I know of which resembles love deep within has been eradicated and all that is left is ashes of my burned heart. The thoughts in my mind as opposed to how it was before the brutal heartache reached my wellbeing is totally futile!

I have lost control of my life on this Earth and the only thing that is left in me is a stung sentiment without any means of being repaired. My eyes turned dark red due to an overflow of tears from the pain caused by my soul mate. The termination of our communication has left me feeling empty as a nutshell.

I miss the old good days whereby forever was perceived every minute we exchanged tête-à-têtes. I remain outside the doorsteps waiting to enter the warm place specially created for us by God. My bad behavior gave me nothing, but took away everything I lived for. I beg for thee to accept me back because I am dying outside due to the cold winter breeze I'm enduring due to being outside Karise's heart.

Days are sweet while some are sour, our paramount aspirations never cease to reach us abundantly. However, we are blessed with more than what we bargained for because God takes away what we want and offers what we are destined for. Even though I SHOULD HAVE BEEN SIX FEET UNDER, I still appreciate days along with its times of the day until mini-seconds. Those who hurt me at first exchanging tête-à-têtes with them was like walking in a world of candies.

To all bliss firmaments I am delighted to have come across those lassies existence. A life altering scenario was when I first glanced into their lozenge eyes and got attached. Meeting new people is a challenge that we ought to get through and knowing all the women I encountered makes me dare to wish they were the finish line in this long search of Ms. Right.

The greatest reward I ever got for my life was knowing how to overcome heartache through all kinds of trauma and endlessly I shall apprize the gift that I am blessed with.

Red roses along with its aroma smell in the garden, the brightness of the morning sun offering light in the dawn, the midnight diamonds offering light in the night all compared to my presence in my life serve little importance.

After everything is all said and done, I welcome the world into the world of Sensational Lummitor, a place of worshipping the conditions of the sentiment. I introduce souls to the world of always being a fighter instead of a loser at all circumstances.

Excruciating pain deep within the heart is brought to an end, the souls living under the dark begins to see the light. A smile is brought back to the saddened ones, welcome to the world of Sensational Lummitor whereby I hold all the keys to this wonderful kingdom. God's grace opened the gates long before you came knocking, the heaven skies made me a doctor to my heart and I am the only one who can allow or neglect what goes into it.

I invite you all to the house of sensational. A so called place full of candies and remedy to the soul. Due to my unbelievable pain I have become a doctor assigned to heal the broken hearts across the world.

EVEN THOUGH I THOUGHT I SHOULD HAVE BEEN SIX FEET UNDER LONG BACK, I AM GRATEFUL THAT FATE PROVED ME WRONG.